DISNEP · PIXAR
THE WORLD OF

Cars

"DIRTY JOB"

RADIATOR S___
IS LOOKING ___
NOW, **SALLY**!

D0561769

EXCEPT FOR OUR POOR LITTLE MURAL...

IT'S IN **REALLY** BAD SHAPE! THE PAINT IS PEELING OFF...

HEY! WHAT'S WRONG WITH PEELING PAINT?

UH...NOT **YOU**, MATER. I MEAN...UH...

JUST KIDDING, BUDDY!

HEY, I'VE GOT AN IDEA. LET'S PAINT A **NEW** ONE!

HEY, MAN, I'M ALL FOR IT!

BAH! WHAT'S WRONG WITH THE **OLD** ONE?

HUH?

WRITER: ALESSANDRO SISTI   PENCILS: VALENTINO FORLINI   INKS: SONIA MATRONE   COLORS: GIORGIO VALLORANI   LETTERS: MICHAEL STEWART

1

IT'S FINE! IT JUST NEEDS--

COME ON, *DOC!* DON'T BE SUCH A *GRUMP!*

DO YOU THINK *STANLEY* LIKES LOOKING AT THIS OLD THING ALL DAY?

IT WOULD BE UNPATRIOTIC *NOT* TO REPAINT IT!

IT WOULD BE GOOD FOR BUSINESS!

WE'VE *GOTTA* PAINT ANOTHER ONE!

WHAT DO *YOU* SAY, SALLY?

RAMONE CAN DO IT!

MY HUSBAND IS THE BEST ARTIST AROUND.

YOU CAN COUNT ON ME!

WELL, UH... I AGREE WITH THEM!

3

RAMONE, CAN YOU ADD SOME BUMBLEBEES?

I LIKE BUMBLEBEES.

PUT IN SOMETHING THAT WILL LET PEOPLE KNOW THIS IS A PLACE OF PEACE AND ORGANIC LIVING.

BUT *ALSO* A PLACE OF PATRIOTS AND GOOD MORALS!

≶GROAN≶

OK, IF YOU KNOW IT ALL, WHY DON'T *YOU* HELP ME?

GIVE ME SOME PAINT, HOTSHOT!

I'LL HELP YA, HONEY!

THERE CAN NEVER BE TOO MANY FLOWERS!

AND *STARS!*

AND A LOT OF *RED, WHITE, AND BLUE!*

ART WAS BETTER BACK IN THE '20S!

BETTER MAKE THINGS CLEAR FROM THE START.

DONE!

ISN'T IT A BEAUTY!

WELL...

¿UGH? IT'S KIND OF A MESS...

¿SIGH? IT LOOKS *WORSE* THAN BEFORE!

HEY, MAYBE WHEN IT DRIES IT WILL LOOK DIFFERENT!

WRITER: CARLOTTA QUATTROCOLO   PENCILS: VALENTINO FORLINI   INKS: SONIA MATRONE   COLOR: VALENTINO FORLINI   LETTERS: JOHN GREEN

7

DON'T WORRY! I'M GREAT AT PLANNING DATES! UHM... YOU COULD TAKE HER FISHING...

I CAUGHT... SOMETHING?

YOU MIGHT EVEN FIND MY *HOOD*!

OR YOU COULD GO *TRACTOR TIPPING*...

SO *THIS* IS THE PLAN FOR THE EVENING?

UHM... MATER *ALWAYS* HAS FUN DOING THIS...

OR...

ACTUALLY, MATER, I THINK WE'LL JUST GO FOR A DRIVE AND POP IN AT FLO'S!

HUH? WAIT! WHAT ABOUT A LITTLE *DIRT* RACING?

THE END!

WHAT DO **YOU** THINK, DOC? IS THIS OLD PLACE WORTH **FIXING UP?**

WHY BOTHER? THEY JUST **DON'T** MAKE MOVIES LIKE THEY USED TO.

YEAH, NOW THEY HAVE ALL THAT **EXTRA** STUFF IN THEM--LIKE **SOUND** AND **COLOR.**

DON'T WORRY, SALLY.

MCQUEEN WILL THINK OF SOMETHIN'. RIGHT, BUDDY?

UH, YEAH. YEAH. DON'T WORRY, SALLY, I'VE GOT IT COVERED!

THANKS, STICKERS.

SOON...

MATER, I DON'T **HAVE A** PLAN TO CLEAR THE DRIVE-IN!

WELL, I'M SURE WE CAN THINK OF **SOMETHIN'**... I KNOW!

WE'LL GET BESSIE AND SOME OLD GAS CANS, AND WE'LL TUNNEL UNDER...

≶SIGH≶

WELL, HONK MY HORN! IT'S OUR **LUCKY DAY,** LIGHTNIN'!

THERE'S OUR PLAN RIGHT THERE. AND IT'LL BE FUU-**UN!**

HUH? ALL I SEE ARE **TRACTORS...**

14

WRITER: ALESSANDRO SISTI   PENCILS: VALENTINO FORLINI   INKS: RAFFAELLA SECCIA   COLOR: VALENTINO FORLINI   LETTERS: JOHN GREEN

YOU CAN SEE FOR YOURSELF. I'M *ARRESTING MCQUEEN!*

WHAT FOR? WHAT DID HE DO WRONG?

I DON'T KNOW WHAT'S GOTTEN INTO DOC, BUT HE WENT THROUGH HIS OLD *LAW BOOK...*

"...AND DISCOVERED A BUNCH OF FORGOTTEN LOCAL RULES."

A-HA!

LIKE CODE 6906--IT IS *PROHIBITED* IN RADIATOR SPRINGS TO DRIVE WITHOUT *HEADLIGHTS* AND A *HORN!*

APPARENTLY MY HEADLIGHT STICKERS DON'T COUNT, AND I DON'T HAVE A HORN.

PLUS, CODE 61006-- HIS ENGINE IS *TOO POWERFUL...* AND PLENTY OF OTHER DETAILS.

SO DOC HAS DECIDED TO PUT HIM ON *TRIAL* IMMEDIATELY!

THAT'S CRAZY!

SOON . . .

IT MAY BE CRAZY, BUT IT'S THE *LAW!*

THEN *I'LL* DEFEND HIM.

IMPOSSIBLE! YOU'RE THE PROSECUTOR.

NOT THIS TIME.

I CAN REPLACE YOU, HONEY!

ORDER IN THE COURT! SALLY, DON'T MAKE ME CHARGE YOU WITH CONTEMPT. *LIZZIE*, TAKE YOUR PLACE WITH THE ACCUSED.

LET THE TRIAL BEGIN.

MATER? DO YOU HEAR SOME HOTROD SPEEDERS OUT THERE?

UM, YEAH... WE BETTER GO CATCH 'EM. LET'S GO!

I DON'T BELIEVE THIS. THIS IS CRAZY, *DOC!* HE CAN'T HAVE A FAIR TRIAL UNDER THESE CONDITIONS. IF YOU WANT TO TALK LAW CODES, THEN...

COME ON, QUICK!

THEY'LL BE THERE FOR A WHILE.

MEANWHILE...

DOES THE DEFENDANT PLEAD *GUILTY* OR *INNOCENT*?

IF ONLY STANLEY WERE HERE, YOU'D ANSWER HIM!

WHAT SORT OF A QUESTION IS *THAT*, DOC?

I REMEMBER EYEING STANLEY FROM ACROSS THE COURTROOM. HE WAS A HANDSOME DEVIL...

LIZZIE? STAY *WITH* ME HERE...

ONCE HE ASKED ME TO BE HIS DATE AT A PARTY. HEY, WHEN IS THAT *PARTY* ANYWAY?

PARTY? WHAT PARTY?

LIZZIE MEANT IT WOULD BE A REAL *PARTY* FOR CRIMINALS IF THE LAW WERE NOT RESPECTED!

OF COURSE! EXACTLY!

ELSEWHERE...

GRAND OPENING

LET'S HURRY UP!

THE TRIAL WON'T LAST FOREVER!

IN FACT...

DOC! LOOK!

UH... WELL, THE COURT CLOSES AT 4 O'CLOCK. TIME'S UP.

THE CASE IS CLOSED! I PRONOUNCE THE DEFENDANT... GUILTY!

WHAAAT?!?

YOU'RE WRONG! I WON'T STAND FOR THIS!

CLANG!

IF YOU WANT TO THROW ME IN JAIL, YOU'LL HAVE TO CATCH ME FIRST!

QUICK, LET'S FOLLOW HIM!

WAIT FOR ME!

WHERE ARE THEY GOING? IT LOOKS LIKE THEY'RE HEADING...

...TOWARD THE WHEEL WELL?

FOR SHE'S A JOLLY GOOD FELLOW, FOR SHE'S...

DID YOU FORGET WHAT DAY IT IS TODAY?

OH? I...

IT'S THE *ANNIVERSARY* OF YOUR ARRIVAL IN RADIATOR SPRINGS!

AT THE SPOT YOU LOVE THE MOST-- WHICH WAS RIGHT HERE.

TO DECORATE IT PROPERLY!

SO YOU SET UP THAT FAKE TRIAL? WHOSE IDEA WAS IT?

HEY, MY ACTING WAS PRETTY GOOD, HUH? MCQUEEN, YOU THINK I COULD GET A PART IN ONE OF THOSE BIG MOVIES?

SINCE I AM THE JUDGE, I CAN CONFESS... WE ARE *ALL* GUILTY!

MATER...

THE END!

Rust-eze
Bumper

...THE GREAT RACE CAR *LIGHTNING MCQUEEN* IS NOW STARTING THE LAST LAP AT THE HEAD OF THE RACE.

START

IT LOOKS LIKE NOTHING CAN STOP HIM FROM WINNING, RIGHT, BOB?

YOU'RE RIGHT, DARRELL--MCQUEEN IS SIMPLY *UNBEATABLE* TODAY, BUT...

... HOLD ON, NOW! WHAT'S GOING ON?

?

I CAN'T BELIEVE MY WINDSCREEN, BOB! MCQUEEN IS GOING IN THE *OPPOSITE* DIRECTION!

START

VRROOOONNNN

IT'S *INCREDIBLE!* EVERYONE IS OVERTAKING HIM. HE'LL END UP *LOSING* . . .

WRITER: ALESSANDRO FERRARI   PENCILS: VALENTINO FORLINI   INKS: SONIA MATRONE   COLORS: VALENTINO FORLINI   LETTERS: JOHN GREEN

BUT... WHAT ARE YOU DOING? WHERE ARE YOU *GOING?*

VRROOOOONNN

HOW COULD HE FORGET THAT THE LAST LAP IS RUN IN *REVERSE?*

I DON'T KNOW, BOB, BUT I DO KNOW THAT LIGHTNING MCQUEEN'S BRILLIANT CAREER HAS MET WITH A *DEFEAT* TODAY!

NO... NO... *NO!*

WOW...

...IT WAS JUST A DREAM. I REALLY HAVE TO STOP THAT BACKWARDS DRIVING WITH *MATER!*

SPEAKING OF MATER, I'M HAVING BREAKFAST WITH HIM AND SALLY AT FLO'S AND I'M ALREADY LATE!

GOOD THING THAT DRIVING IN THE RIGHT DIRECTION IS THE THING I KNOW HOW TO DO BEST.

NO... IT'S IMPOSSIBLE... THIS IS A *NIGHTMARE!*

SKREEE

I MUST STILL BE DREAMING-- THANKS TO MATER AND HIS BACKWARDS DRIVING!

WHERE ARE YOU GOING?

I'M GOING BACK TO *SLEEP!* SEE YOU WHEN I WAKE UP... *AGAIN!*

VROOM

HEY, DID YOU HEAR THAT, HE THANKED ME! HE REALLY LIKED THE *JOKE,* DIDN'T HE, SALLY?

I'M NOT SO SURE, MATER . . . MAYBE THAT WASN'T SO FUNNY AFTER ALL!

THE END!